THE STORY OF THE
MINNESOTA TWINS

SEC.
14

ROW
8

SEAT
10

GRANDSTAND SEAT $6.00
Est. Price $5.00 · Tax $1.00 · TOTAL

GAME
4

Right hereby reserved to refund said price
and revoke license granted by this ticket.

DAY GAME
THE BALLPARK
★ ★
American League
vs.
National League

GAME
4

Read Important
Notices on
Reverse Side
★
Do Not Detach
This Coupon From
Rain Check

RAIN CHECK

DAY GAME

GRANDSTAND SEAT
Est. Price $5.00 $6.00
Fed. Tax $1.00
TOTAL

GAME
4

Right hereby reserved to refund said price and revoke
license granted by this ticket.

**READ IMPORTANT NOTICES
ON REVERSE SIDE**

SEC.
14

ROW
8

SEAT
10

Published by Creative Education
P.O. Box 227, Mankato, Minnesota 56002
Creative Education is an imprint of The Creative Company

Design and production by Blue Design
Printed in the United States of America

Photographs by Corbis (Bettmann, Minnesota Historical Society, Brian Snyder/Reuters), Getty Images (Diamond Images, Stephen Dunn, Focus on Sport, Otto Greule Jr, Judy Griesedieck//Time Life Pictures, Robert Leiter/MLB Photos, MLB Photos, National Baseball Hall of Fame Library/MLB Photos, Anthony Neste//Time Life Pictures, Tom Pidgeon, Rich Pilling/MLB Photos, Bill Polo/MLB Photos, Louis Requena/MLB Photos, Herb Scharfman/Sports Imagery, Gregory Shamus, Jon SooHoo/MLB Photos, Tony Tomsic/MLB Photos, Ron Vesely/MLB Photos, Hank Walker//Time Life Pictures, John Williamson/MLB Photos, Alex Wong, Michael Zagaris/MLB Photos)

Library of Congress Cataloging-in-Publication Data

LeBoutillier, Nate.
The story of the Minnesota Twins / by Nate LeBoutillier.
p. cm. — (Baseball: the great American game)
Includes index.
ISB-13: 978-1-58341-493-4
1. Minnesota Twins (Baseball team)—History—Juvenile literature. I. Title. II. Series.

GV875.M55L43 2007
796.357'6409776579—dc22   2006018255

First Edition
9 8 7 6 5 4 3 2 1

Cover: First baseman Justin Morneau
Page 1: Outfielder Tony Oliva
Page 3: Pitcher Johan Santana

THE STORY OF THE
MINNESOTA TWINS

by Nate LeBoutillier

KIRBY PUCKETT

Minnesota Twins

I t's the third inning of Game 6 of the 1991 World Series in the Metrodome, and Minnesota Twins center fielder Kirby Puckett's back is up against the wall, literally. Outfielder Ron Gant of the Atlanta Braves has just knocked a towering fly ball to deep center field, trying to bring his team one step closer to turning a three-games-to-two series lead into a World Series-clinching win. But Puckett has other ideas. His squat, 5-foot-9 frame drifts back to the warning track, and then he leaps impos-

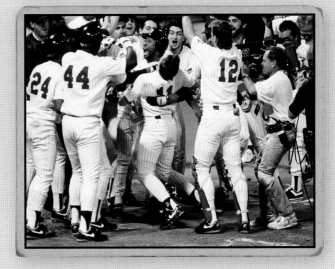

sibly high and extends his glove against the Plexiglas wall to snare Gant's blast, stealing a sure extra-base hit. But Puckett's work is not done. In the bottom of the 11th inning, he bashes a game-winning homer into left-center field, forcing a Game 7. The Twins will win the World Series in Game 7, and Puckett will go down as the greatest all-around player in Twins history.

TWINS ORIGINS

Like two friends from different sides of the train tracks, Minneapolis and St. Paul make a divergent yet complementary pair. Minneapolis hosts a burgeoning population and plays the part of the ever-changing, more modern city on the rise, while St. Paul houses the state's capitol and boasts a rich history embodied by its many majestic brick buildings. The mighty Mississippi River flows between the two cities, and the metropolitan area around them includes nearly three million of Minnesota's five million residents.

Baseball history in the "Twin Cities" dates back to the 1870s, when local teams named the Minneapolis Millers and the St. Paul Saints started play. But it wasn't until 1961 that Major League Baseball came to Minnesota. Founded in 1901 in Washington, D.C., a franchise known as the Washington Senators won the 1924 World Series but steadily declined thereafter. Fan attendance waned as the losses mounted, and in 1961, team owner Calvin Griffith announced that the team would relocate to the Twin Cities, where it would get a new start as the Minnesota Twins.

The Twins featured several fine young players during their early years. A stocky, muscular slugger named Harmon Killebrew wielded a lumberjack's swing that

A humble star nicknamed "The Killer," Harmon Killebrew was the league's top slugger in the 1960s.

HARMON KILLEBREW

produced towering home run blasts. Each year from 1962 to 1964, "The Killer" led the American League (AL) in home runs. Right fielder Tony Oliva, who won 1964 AL Rookie of the Year honors, peppered pitches to any part of the field. Left fielder Bobby Allison provided long-ball power as well, and with the additional hard hitting of shortstop Zoilo Versalles and catcher Earl Battey, the Twins swung a loaded bat. On the pitching mound, Minnesota boasted such fine hurlers as Jim "Mudcat" Grant and Jim Kaat, the all-time winningest pitcher in club history.

TONY OLIVA – Oliva excelled at almost every phase of the game. He became the first player ever to win league batting titles in his first two full big-league seasons (1964 and 1965), and in 1966 he won a Gold Glove award for his great defensive play.

TONY OLIVA

MILLERS AND SAINTS

Baseball history is rich in Minnesota, dating back to the post-Civil War baseball boom of the 1870s. By 1884, the Northwestern League contained many teams, two of which were located in Minneapolis and St. Paul. The Western League—which would later become the modern-day American League—was founded in the 1890s, and it featured the Minneapolis Millers and St. Paul Saints. In 1902, the Saints and Millers became charter members of the American Association, a minor league that would feature the two teams until the Minnesota Twins came to town in 1961. The Millers and Saints played 22 inter-city games each summer, and on the holidays of Decoration Day, the Fourth of July, and Labor Day, a double-header would be played that included a morning game in either Lexington Park in St. Paul or Nicollet Park in Minneapolis, a streetcar ride across the mighty Mississippi River, and then an afternoon game in the opposite ballpark. Many great players competed for the Millers and Saints on their way to the major leagues, including Ted Williams, Willie Mays, Duke Snider, and Roy Campanella. In all, 21 players now enshrined in the Baseball Hall of Fame once played for either the Millers or the Saints.

PITCHER · BERT BLYLEVEN

A reliable starter with a baffling curveball, Blyleven played 22 major-league seasons and won 287 games. Ten and a half of those seasons and 139 of those wins were with Minnesota. A man with a great sense of humor, Blyleven could both take it and dish it out. Teammates who would tease him about the high number of home runs he gave up (he led the major leagues in 1986 and 1987) might find themselves with a whipped cream pie in their face during a TV interview, courtesy of Blyleven. Since 1995, he has worked as a color commentator on Twins television broadcasts.

STATS

Twins seasons: 1970–76, 1985–88

Height: 6-3

Weight: 205

- **60 career complete-game shutouts**

- **287–250 career record**

- **3,701 career strikeouts**

- **2-time All-Star**

BERT BLYLEVEN
PITCHER

MINNESOTA
TWINS

The Twins were a juggernaut by 1965, posting a 102–60 record. Leading the way were AL Most Valuable Player (MVP) Versalles, league batting champ Oliva, and the feared Killebrew. Fans came in league-leading droves to Metropolitan Stadium in the suburb of Bloomington and cheered as their squad roared all the way to the pennant, securing a berth in the World Series.

In the World Series, the Twins met the mighty Los Angeles Dodgers, seasoned winners of three World Series, and runners-up in many other postseason battles with the New York Yankees. The Twins and Dodgers fought to a split after the first six games, and it all came down to one last game. But in Game 7, Sandy Koufax, the Dodgers' ace pitcher with the blazing fastball, shut the Twins out 2–0 to give Los Angeles the championship. "You hate to lose, but we didn't disgrace ourselves," said Twins manager Sam Mele. "We were beaten by the best pitcher that there is anywhere."

JIM KAAT

Famous for his superb fielding, Jim Kaat built a major-league career that ran from the 1950s to the '80s.

FOILED BY THE ORIOLES

Despite the World Series loss, Minnesota fans were confident that their slugging Twins would get another shot at the title. In a 1966 game versus the Kansas City Royals, the Twins set a major-league record when five players hit home runs in the same inning! However, the 1966 Twins finished a distant second to the powerful Baltimore Orioles, who went on to best the Dodgers in the World Series.

The Twins bolstered their lineup even further in 1967 with the addition of rookie second baseman Rod Carew. Pitchers found the young Carew to be one tough out as he slapped hit after hit en route to the AL Rookie of the Year award. "Rod Carew could get more hits with a soup bone than I could get with a rack full of bats," said Twins outfielder Steve Brye.

The Twins went 91–71 in 1967, but the Boston Red Sox squeaked by them by a single game to take the pennant. The team was a disappointment in 1968, but the same core of players that nearly won the 1965 World Series would give it one last push over the next two seasons. Major League Baseball decided to split the American and National Leagues into two divisions apiece in 1969, and Minnesota landed in the AL Western Division. Twins fans were thankful to see the team's nemesis, Baltimore, designated to the AL East.

ROD CAREW – In a 12-year Twins career, Carew led the league in batting average a whopping 7 times. Heavy on speed and skill but light on long-ball power, he became, in 1972, the first AL player ever to win a batting title without hitting a home run.

CATCHER · **EARL BATTEY**

Spending 7 of his 13 big-league seasons with the Twins, Battey was the solid battery mate for talented pitchers such as Camilo Pascual, Jim "Mudcat" Grant, Jim Kaat, and Jim Perry in the 1960s. A reliable hitter whose batting average always hovered near the .300 mark, Battey was no slouch behind the plate either. A four-time All-Star and the winner of three Gold Glove awards, Battey was equally adept at handling balls in the dirt and gunning down base runners. And in an era where catchers called the pitches rather than the managers, Battey called a clever game.

STATS

Twins seasons: 1960 (Washington Senators), 1961–67

Height: 6-1

Weight: 205

- **104 career HR**
- **449 career RBI**
- **3-time Gold Glove winner**
- **4-time All-Star**

EARL BATTEY
CATCHER

MINNESOTA
TWINS

CESAR TOVAR

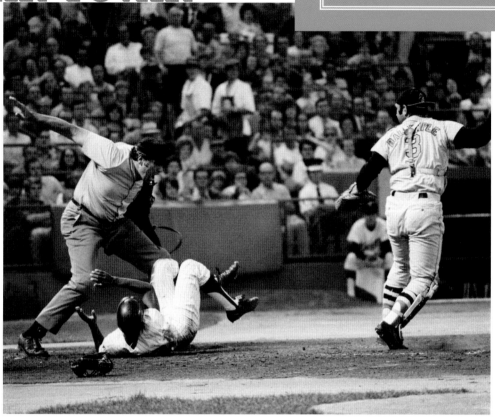

New pitcher Dave Boswell and holdover Jim Perry each won 20 games for the Twins in 1969, and outfielder Cesar Tovar teamed up with Carew, Oliva, and 1969 AL MVP Killebrew to pace the offense. But despite winning the AL West in both 1969 and 1970, the Twins were swept in the playoffs by the Orioles each time. "We had some great ballclubs back then," Killebrew later said, "but Baltimore always had our number."

The 1970 season was Minnesota's last hurrah for a while, and the Twins hovered near the .500 mark throughout the 1970s, turning in solid but unspectacular performances. Fans bid farewell to several longtime Twins heroes as Killebrew's career wound down and Oliva succumbed to knee problems. Seventeen seasons would pass after the Twins' postseason battles with Baltimore before Minnesota fans would taste playoff excitement again.

Carew won the AL MVP award in 1977, and pitcher Bert Blyleven threw a curveball that bent crazily, baffling many an opposing batter in the late 1970s. But Twins owner Calvin Griffith, saddled with financial problems, then replaced the majority of the ballclub's highly paid veterans—including Carew and Blyleven—with younger, less expensive players.

The Twins celebrated 20 years of baseball in Minnesota in 1981 by finishing dead last in the AL West, and fan attendance at Met Stadium dropped to new lows. Second baseman John Castino led Twins hitters with a paltry .268 batting average, shortstop Roy Smalley was the team's top home run hitter with just seven dingers, and the most wins a Twins pitcher could muster was nine, recorded by Pete Redfern.

FIRST BASEMAN · KENT HRBEK

A homegrown standout, this Bloomington, Minnesota, native was a solid fixture at first base for the Twins for more than a decade. In his first game in a Twins uniform, Hrbek hit a game-winning homer in the 12th inning. The 1982 All-Star and runner-up for AL Rookie of the Year was also an avid outdoorsman, hunting and fishing when his baseball schedule permitted. Hrbek played a big role in boosting the Twins to World Series titles in 1987 and 1991, with a key highlight being a Game 6 grand slam against the Cardinals in 1987 that helped win the game, 11–5.

KENT HRBEK
FIRST BASEMAN

MINNESOTA
TWINS

STATS

Twins seasons: 1981–94

Height: 6-4

Weight: 260

- **.282 career BA**

- **293 career HR**

- **1,086 career RBI**

- **Uniform number (14) retired by Twins**

TOM BRUNANSKY

TWIN TURNAROUND

The Twins set franchise records for losing in 1982 with a 14-game losing streak and a 60–102 final mark, but that season marked a changing of the guard. The team moved into the Hubert H. Humphrey Metrodome—an indoor stadium with a Teflon roof that looked like a big bubble—in downtown Minneapolis, and new heroes emerged.

Rookie first baseman Kent Hrbek, a Minnesota boy with the chest of a bear but the reflexes of a cat, batted .301 in 1982 and was named an All-Star. Hard-hitting Gary Gaetti played third base with dirty-uniform grit, and right fielder Tom Brunansky wielded a booming bat. Joining the pitching staff was crafty left-hander Frank Viola. The Twins floundered again in 1982, but something was building.

In 1982, the Twins also drafted Kirby Puckett, a round, 5-foot-9 third baseman. Puckett broke into the Twins' starting lineup in 1984 as an outfielder, and his nonstop hustle and ever-present smile quickly endeared him to Minnesota baseball enthusiasts. Of course, it didn't hurt that Puckett tracked down fly balls in center field with a sure glove and lashed line drives all over the

Tom Brunansky brought steady power to the plate, hitting 20 or more homers every season from 1982 to 1989.

DOME FIELD ADVANTAGE

From raised to lowered pitching mounds, eccentric outfield walls, or peculiar foul territories, major league baseball teams are constantly looking for a home field advantage. When the Twins began playing their home games in the Hubert H. Humphrey Metrodome in Minneapolis in 1982, becoming just the third team to play under an artificial sky (the Houston Astros and the Seattle Mariners were the first two), they acquired a ballpark full of quirks. Opposing players often complained of losing track of fly balls due to the baseball-colored roof, batted balls would skip and bounce off the artificial turf as if they were toy superballs, and, occasionally, high popups would deflect off of hanging speakers (which were deemed "in play") or even the rooftop itself. In 2003, Dick Ericson, a Dome groundskeeper from 1982 to 1995, made the strange admittance that he sometimes turned the air conditioning on and off during games in the hopes of affecting the flight of baseballs to the Twins' advantage. "I became very suspicious, maybe paranoid," said Bobby Valentine, former manager of the Texas Rangers. "They had such an uncanny way of winning." Twins officials claimed they had no knowledge of the air being manipulated.

diamond. "Scouts would always tell me I was too short, or too heavy, or too whatever," said Puckett. "But baseball isn't about being a shape or a size. It's about how big you are inside that counts."

In 1986, Puckett helped give Minnesota a powerful offense. Unfortunately, the team's pitching was weak, and the Twins sank back into last place with a 71–91 record. Late in that season, however, Minnesota made a pivotal move, hiring 36-year-old Tom Kelly as the youngest manager in the major leagues. Under Kelly's stoic guidance, the Twins quickly improved.

Viola and veteran Bert Blyleven (back in a Minnesota uniform for a second stint) headed up the pitching crew in 1987, combining for 32 wins, and closer Jeff Reardon racked up 31 saves. Meanwhile, Hrbek, Puckett, Gaetti, and Brunansky each slugged at least 28 homers as the upstart Twins won the 1987 AL West crown with an 85–77 record. "We just do what T.K. [Kelly] tells us," Puckett explained. "Don't get too high, don't get too low. Just go out, give 100 percent, and we'll win the battle one game at a time."

In the 1987 AL Championship Series (ALCS), the Twins toppled the team with the best record in the majors, the Detroit Tigers, four games to one. For the first time in 22 years, the Twins were going to the World Series. Just as in 1965, the Twins of 1987 were considered underdogs—this time to St. Louis's mighty Cardinals. But the Twins surprised the experts by crushing the Cardinals 10–1 and 8–4 in front of earsplitting Metrodome crowds in the first two games.

GARY GAETTI

One of the Twins' most popular players, third baseman Gary Gaetti made the AL All-Star team in 1987 and 1989.

SECOND BASEMAN · ROD CAREW

With a quick bat and lightning speed on the base paths, Carew burst upon the major-league scene in 1967, batting .292 and winning Rookie of the Year honors. Never much of a power hitter, Carew was content to cock his bat back only halfway and flick it rather than really swing it, which let him slap the ball to all fields and use his lively legs. Carew was most famous for stealing home plate seven times in 1969, a major-league record. Although Carew's 3,000th career hit came as a member of the California Angels, he got it against, fittingly, the Twins.

STATS

Twins seasons: 1967–78

Height: 6-0

Weight: 180

- **.328 career BA**
- **18-time All-Star**
- **Uniform number (29) retired by Twins**
- **Baseball Hall of Fame inductee (1991)**

ROD CAREW
SECOND BASEMAN

MINNESOTA
TWINS

FRANK VIOLA

Frank Viola's deceptive changeup pitch made him a 1987 World Series hero and the 1988 Cy Young Award winner.

St. Louis won the next three games in a row at their home ballpark, Busch Stadium, taking the series lead back to the Dome. Minnesota's offense roared in an 11–5 Game 6 win, setting up a dramatic Game 7. Viola took the mound for the Twins and lived up to his nickname of "Sweet Music," fooling Cardinals hitters with his masterful "circle changeup" pitch and surrendering only six hits as the Twins won 4–2 to take home the World Series championship trophy. "We're no longer the Twinkies," said Twins second baseman Steve Lombardozzi, referring to critics who, during Minnesota's losing years, nicknamed the Twins after the soft, cream-filled confection. "We are the world champion Minnesota Twins."

Bert Blyleven played for five big-league teams but spent most of his finest seasons in a Twins uniform.

BERT BLYLEVEN

THE WONDERS OF A GAME 7

There's nothing like the drama of playing in a Game 7 for a championship. The Twins have been fortunate enough to have been involved in three World Series Game 7s. The 1965 Game 7 featured two dominant southpaw pitchers, Minnesota's Jim Kaat and the Los Angeles Dodgers' legendary ace, Sandy Koufax. Fighting chronic arm pain, Koufax started Game 7 on just two days' rest yet pitched a three-hit shutout in the Dodgers' 2–0 win. In 1987's Game 7, the Twins relied on their "10th man"—the screaming, handkerchief-waving Metrodome crowd—and the pitching of Frank Viola to earn a 4–2 win over the St. Louis Cardinals. Jack Morris was the hero in the Twins' 1991 Game 7 victory, pitching 10 shutout innings to best Atlanta Braves pitcher John Smoltz, who pitched a scoreless nine innings only to watch the Twins win in the bottom of the 10th, when they scored the game's lone run. "You feel so numb that you could go in for surgery and not need any anesthetic," said Twins outfielder Tom Brunansky in 1987 after the thrilling Game 7 win. "The sprint to the pile, the jumping on everybody—you don't feel your feet touching the ground."

THIRD BASEMAN · HARMON KILLEBREW

At age 18, Killebrew was the youngest player in the major leagues when he broke into the Washington Senators' lineup in 1954. "The Killer" never once topped .300 in his 14 seasons of service in Minnesota, but hitting for average wasn't Killebrew's game—hitting the long ball was. In 1967, he hit the longest home run (520 feet) in Twins history. Killebrew walloped the homer into the sixth row of the upper deck of Metropolitan Stadium, cracking the seat, which was later painted a commemorative orange. He holds many of the Twins' franchise records for longevity, including games played (1,939).

STATS

Twins seasons: 1954–60 (Washington Senators), 1961–74

Height: 5-11

Weight: 215

- **573 career HR**
- **1,584 career RBI**
- **Uniform number (3) retired by Twins**
- **Baseball Hall of Fame inductee (1984)**

HARMON KILLEBREW
THIRD BASEMAN

MINNESOTA
TWINS

THE BEST SERIES EVER?

y 1990, the Twins had stumbled back into last place with a 74–88 record. Blyleven and Viola had been traded away, and Minnesota's young pitchers struggled. "We just aren't getting it done on the mound," said Kelly. "But hopefully the lumps we take now will pay off down the road."

Minnesota sputtered early in 1991 but caught fire in June, winning a franchise-best 15 straight games. Pitcher Scott Erickson led the AL with 20 wins on the season, and the rebuilt pitching staff featured Kevin Tapani, veteran Jack Morris, and reliever Rick Aguilera. Key additions to the offense were slugging designated hitter Chili Davis and hustling second baseman Chuck Knoblauch, who captured the 1991 AL Rookie of the Year award.

The Twins finished atop their division with a 95–67 mark and trounced the Toronto Blue Jays in the ALCS, four games to one. Just as in 1987, the 1991 Twins had gone from worst to first in their division and fought their way to the World Series. This time they met the Atlanta Braves, another "Cinderella" team that had also finished in last place in its division the previous season.

The 1991 World Series played out in epic fashion, going seven nail-biting games—five of which were decided by a single run. As in 1987, the Twins won

JACK MORRIS

JACK MORRIS – As a member of the Detroit Tigers, Morris became baseball's winningest pitcher of the 1980s before joining the Twins in 1991. He spent just one season in Minnesota but became a local legend with his brilliant World Series effort.

the first two games in the Metrodome but lost the next three on the road. With Minnesota facing elimination, Puckett dominated Game 6, making a spectacular leaping catch in the third inning and knocking an 11th-inning pitch into the stands to win the game and extend the series.

Game 7 pitted Morris, a St. Paul native, against Braves ace John Smoltz. Each was outstanding, and the game remained scoreless after nine innings. Kelly told Morris he intended to bring in a reliever in the 10th, but the hot-tempered hurler insisted on returning to the mound. "I would have needed a shotgun to get him out of the game," said Kelly. "And I didn't have one."

Morris pitched a clean 10th inning, and it would be all the Twins would need. In the bottom of the 10th, Minnesota loaded the bases, and then pinch

TRIPLE THE FUN, TWICE

The triple play in baseball is a rare event, and since the Twins started playing in Minnesota in 1961, the team has turned just 10. But on July 17, 1990, at Boston's legendary Fenway Park in a game versus the Red Sox, the Twins turned not one but two triple plays in the same game. In more than 100 years of professional baseball in America, such a feat had never been accomplished. The first triple play occurred in the fourth inning, when former Twins outfielder Tom Brunansky came to bat for the Red Sox with men on first and second. Brunansky hit a sharp grounder to Twins third baseman Gary Gaetti, who stepped on third and threw to second baseman Al Newman for the force-out. Newman in turn wheeled and fired to first baseman Kent Hrbek in time to force out Brunansky. In the eighth inning, the Twins turned three in the exact same fashion—Gaetti to Newman to Hrbek—when Red Sox second baseman Jodi Reed hit a rocket to third. Despite the two triple plays, the Twins lost the game by the score of 1–0.

hitter Gene Larkin looped a hit into left field. The Metrodome crowd let loose a frenzied roar as outfielder Dan Gladden stomped on home plate to give Minnesota its second world title. Fay Vincent, the commissioner of baseball, said it best when he noted, "It was probably the greatest World Series ever."

Minnesota's reign atop the baseball world ended the next season when the Twins missed the playoffs. In 1993, the Twins went a disappointing 71–91, the first of what would be eight straight losing seasons. Team owner Carl Pohlad cut the club's payroll, and the organization's pool of talent in the minor leagues was frightfully shallow.

In 1995, power-hitting left fielder Marty Cordova won the AL Rookie of

CHILI DAVIS

Chili Davis posted 93 RBI during the 1991 season, then bashed two homers in the World Series.

SHORTSTOP · ZOILO VERSALLES

The Cuban-born speedster was a blur on the baseball diamond, using his quick reaction time to showcase expansive fielding range from the shortstop position or zipping around the base paths to score lots of runs. As the Twins' leadoff batter in the '60s, Versalles set the table for such power-hitting teammates as Harmon Killebrew, Bobby Allison, and Tony Oliva. In 1965, the free-swinging Versalles led the AL in doubles, triples, runs scored—and strikeouts. His 1965 season won him the first AL MVP award in team history and helped power the Twins to their first World Series.

ZOILO VERSALLES
SHORTSTOP

MINNESOTA
TWINS

STATS

Twins seasons: 1959–60 (Washington Senators), 1961–67

Height: 5-10

Weight: 150

- **95 career HR**

- **3-time AL leader in triples**

- **2-time All-Star**

- **1965 AL MVP**

LEFT FIELDER · BOB ALLISON

In his first major-league season with the Washington Senators in 1959, Allison was voted both Rookie of the Year and an All-Star. He went on to make the All-Star team two more times (1963 and 1964) once the franchise moved to Minnesota. As a fixture in left field for the highly successful Twins of the 1960s, Allison is probably best remembered for a single play he made in Game 2 of the 1965 World Series, a run-saving, back-handed, diving catch. In college, the hard-nosed Allison played fullback for the University of Missouri football team.

BOB ALLISON
LEFT FIELDER

MINNESOTA
TWINS

STATS

Twins seasons: 1958–60 (Washington Senators), 1961–70

Height: 6-4

Weight: 220

- **256 career HR**

- **796 career RBI**

- **1959 AL leader in triples (9)**

- **3-time All-Star**

the Year award. Brad Radke, a control pitcher, also performed admirably, but the losses continued to mount. Then, in spring training before the 1996 season, longtime star Kirby Puckett developed blurred vision in his right eye—a disease called glaucoma—and was forced to retire.

In the mid-1990s, the team was led by several veterans in the twilight of bright careers who returned to spend their final big-league seasons in their native state of Minnesota. These included infielder Paul Molitor, designated hitter Dave Winfield, and catcher Terry Steinbach. Although the Twins continued to lose many games, the players and fans appreciated manager Tom Kelly's approach to coaching. "He concentrates on playing the game right," said Steinbach. "His players run balls out. They hit the cutoff man. They don't showboat or hot dog."

Pohlad slashed the Twins' payroll to a league-low $15 million in 1998, leaving the team with a lineup full of inexperienced youngsters. Then, just when it seemed the Twins were beyond hope, the outlook brightened. In 2001, Puckett and Winfield were inducted into the Baseball Hall of Fame, and the Twins made some shrewd drafts and trades to bulk up their minor-league system's stock. As the team moved into a new century, general manager Terry Ryan built up a low-cost club that would soon surprise the baseball world.

CONTRACTION TO CONTENTION

he scrappy Twins led the AL Central Division (formed in 1994) for much of the 2001 season before finishing second to the Cleveland Indians with an 85–77 record. But Major League Baseball then unveiled a dire threat to the team: contraction. The league was losing money, and the Twins were deemed one of its weakest moneymakers. "All you can do is get ready and prepare like you're going to have a season," Twins center fielder Torii Hunter said of the league's threat to fold the team.

The Twins' legal obligation to play in the Metrodome in 2002 saved them, and the team played that season like it might be its last. New manager Ron Gardenhire, a bench coach for many years under Tom Kelly, coached "small ball"—a brand of baseball that involved manufacturing runs one at a time with timely bunts, shrewd base running, and tough defense.

Likable players such as Hunter, first baseman Doug Meintkiewicz, and third baseman Corey Koskie made nightly highlights with their award-winning defense. Shortstop Cristian Guzman provided speed on the base

BUD SELIG

JESSE VENTURA

CONTRACTION DISTRACTION

In November 2001, Major League Baseball Commissioner Bud Selig announced that 25 of baseball's 30 teams lost money during the 2001 season, leaving the league a large collective debt. At a meeting following the 2001 World Series, team owners voted 28–2 to contract, or eliminate, two teams. The leading candidates were two of the least profitable ballclubs, the Montreal Expos and the Twins. Losing money was one thing, but losing fan loyalty was another. Major League Baseball had been trying to win back fan support since a players' strike in 1994 canceled the World Series, and now it wanted to eliminate two baseball markets. Many fans nationwide weren't buying it, and the backlash

began. Some pointed to owners overpaying players as the reason for the lack of prosperity. "When a .250 hitter can sign a contract for $75 million, I think something is wrong at the top level of baseball that needs to be fixed," said Minnesota governor Jesse Ventura. In court, an injunction was upheld requiring the Twins to play in the Metrodome in 2002. And play the Twins did, winning the AL Central Division. The contraction threats died down as the Twins continued to win, and they faded into memory with the 2006 announcement that a new outdoor ballpark would be built for the club in downtown Minneapolis by 2010.

CENTER FIELDER · KIRBY PUCKETT

What Kirby Puckett lacked in size, he made up for in passion for the game. The 5-foot-9 stick of dynamite played a spectacular center field, trademarking for Twins fans the art of leaping impossibly high above the fence to steal home runs (an art that another Minnesota center fielder, Torii Hunter, would later come to master as well). He was the consummate teammate and positive clubhouse influence, playing each game with a joy usually seen only in kids in the sandlot or city park. The whole baseball world mourned when he died of a stroke in 2006.

STATS

Twins seasons: 1984–95

Height: 5-9

Weight: 220

- **.318 career BA**
- **6-time Gold Glove winner**
- **10-time All-Star**
- **Baseball Hall of Fame inductee (2001)**

KIRBY PUCKETT
CENTER FIELDER

MINNESOTA
TWINS

paths, and pitchers Brad Radke, Eric Milton, and reliever Eddie Guardado made the most of limited run support with crafty pitching to catcher A.J. Pierzynski. Behind these players, Minnesota went 94–67 and won the Central Division to return to the playoffs.

In the 2002 AL Division Series (ALDS), the Twins pulled out a thrilling, three-games-to-two win over the Oakland A's. Pierzynski clouted a three-run, ninth-inning home run in Game 5 in Oakland to seal the series win and put the Twins in the ALCS against the Anaheim Angels, another team with a low payroll. In the ALCS, the slightly higher-budget Angels beat the Twins four games to one and went on to win the World Series.

In 2003, with the threat of contraction behind them, the Twins repeated as AL Central champions but were quickly subdued by the New York Yankees in the ALDS. The 2004 Twins won a third straight AL Central title behind the powerful pitching of closer Joe Nathan and starter Johan Santana. A left-hander from Venezuela with a blazing fastball and a baffling change-up, Santana led the major leagues with 265 strikeouts and posted a 20–6 record. These efforts earned him the prestigious Cy Young Award as the league's best pitcher, an honor that had been bestowed on only two other Twins hurlers (Jim Perry in 1970 and Frank Viola in 1988). But, once again, the Yankees made clear that the Twins still had room to improve, stomping Minnesota three games to one in the ALDS for the second year in a row.

RECORD-BREAKING STINGINESS

Three games, 27 innings, and no runs surrendered. That's what the Twins accomplished in a three-game series against the Kansas City Royals on July 5, 6, and 7, 2004, when Minnesota pitchers Brad Radke, Johan Santana, and Kyle Lohse pitched consecutive complete-game shutouts. On July 5, Radke—best known for his pinpoint control—gave up just four hits to the Royals, struck out four, and issued no walks in a 9–0 win. Santana, the 2004 AL Cy Young Award winner, gave up just three hits and struck out 13 Royals the next night as the Twins won 4–0. The Twins finished the three-game sweep with a 12–0 pounding of the Royals that featured Lohse going the distance on the mound while giving up just six hits and striking out seven. "You don't want to think about trying to get the shutout," said Lohse following the game, "but I knew I didn't want to be the guy who ended this streak." The Twins' record streak was extended to 33 scoreless innings when pitcher Terry Mulholland blanked the Detroit Tigers for six innings on July 8. Tigers catcher Ivan Rodriguez blasted a solo home run in the seventh to finally score on the Twins, but Minnesota won the game.

BRAD RADKE

RIGHT FIELDER · TONY OLIVA

"Tony O" burst onto the major-league scene with a bang, winning the AL Rookie of the Year Award in 1964 and leading the league in batting average. A native of Cuba, Oliva hit for both power and average, and he played a sticky-fingered right field. Throughout the mid-to-late 1960s, Oliva teamed with Harmon Killebrew and Rod Carew to lead the Twins deep into the postseason. Bad knees cut short Oliva's career, which would certainly have been of Hall of Fame caliber had it lasted longer. In 1976, Oliva began a career as a coach and scout for the Twins organization, roles he still plays today.

STATS

Twins seasons: 1962–76

Height: 6-2

Weight: 190

- **.304 career BA**

- **947 career RBI**

- **8-time All-Star**

- **Uniform number (6) retired by Twins**

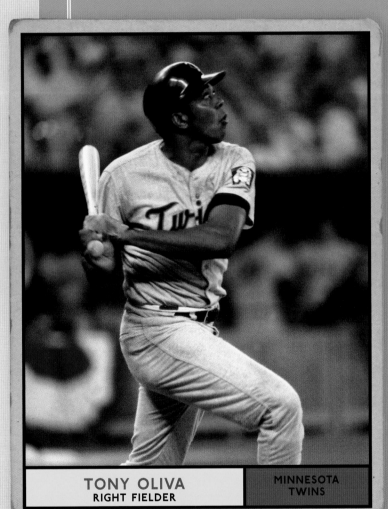

TONY OLIVA
RIGHT FIELDER

MINNESOTA TWINS

TORII HUNTER

Torii Hunter was a human highlight reel in the field, taking away many enemy home runs with spectacular catches.

The Twins put much of their hopes in young players in 2005, namely catcher Joe Mauer and first baseman Justin Morneau, collectively nicknamed the "M&M Boys." Mauer, who grew up in St. Paul, had an arm like a rifle and a sweet left-handed batting stroke. Morneau, meanwhile, was a strapping Canadian who could hit the ball a mile.

The Twins missed the playoffs in 2005 and stumbled early in 2006 before catching fire. Minnesota won 19 of 20 games during one midseason stretch and overtook the Detroit Tigers to win the AL Central title with a 96–66 record on the final day of the season. There were many heroes in the stunning turnaround. Santana was as dominant as ever, winning his second Cy Young Award; rookie pitcher Francisco Liriano earned All-Star status with a 12–3 record before suffering an elbow injury; Mauer hit his way to the AL batting title; and Morneau broke through as a star by putting up 34 homers and 130 runs batted in (RBI) to win the AL MVP award.

Although the celebratory atmosphere in Minnesota ended quickly as the Twins were swept by the Oakland A's in the ALDS, the team and its fans predicted greater playoff success in 2007 and beyond. "We know how to get there," said Gardenhire. "Now, it's just about getting it done when we get there."

Hurling an almost unhittable slider pitch, Francisco Liriano was electrifying in 2006 before being sidelined by injury.

FRANCISCO LIRIANO

MANAGER · TOM KELLY

"T.K." was to the Minnesota Twins what a hot cup of coffee is to a sleepy person in the morning—a sobering, straightforward wake-up call. In 1986, Kelly joined the Twins at age 36, but what he lacked in experience he made up for with a no-nonsense approach to teaching and encouraged his players to play baseball the way it ought to be played—with hustle, heart, and an allegiance to the fundamentals of the game. Prior to managing, the Minnesota native played 49 games for the Twins as a first baseman in 1975, hitting one home run.

TOM KELLY
MANAGER

MINNESOTA
TWINS

STATS

Twins seasons as manager: 1986–2001

Height: 5-11

Weight: 190

Managerial Record: 1,140–1,244

World Series Championships: 1987, 1991

With a history that is rich in talented defensive players such as Kirby Puckett, powerful hitters such as Harmon Killebrew, and masterful pitchers such as Bert Blyleven, the Twins indeed have a tradition to be proud of. And with players such as Joe Mauer and Johan Santana leading the charge into the future, Minnesota baseball fans hope the local boys will soon bring a third world championship to the Twin Cities.

In 2006, rising star Joe Mauer became the first catcher ever to lead the AL in batting average, hitting .347.

JOE MAUER